First published 2021

Published by Forward Thinking Publishing

Text © Katherine Taylor 2021

The moral rights of the author have been asserted.

All rights reserved. No part of this book may be reproduced by any mechanical, photographic or electronic process, or in the form of a phonographic recording; nor may it be stored in a retrieval system, transmitted or otherwise be copied for public or private use, other than for 'fair use' as brief quotations embodied in articles and reviews, without prior written permission of the publisher and author.

The information given in this book should not be treated as a substitute for professional medical advice; always consult a medical practitioner. Any use of information in this book is at the reader's discretion and risk. Neither the author nor the publisher can be held responsible for any loss, claim or damage arising out of the use, or misuse, of the suggestions made, the failure to take medical advice or for any material on third party websites.

A catalogue record for this book is available from the British Library.

ISBN: 978-1-8380445-4-1

Dedication

This book is for Mike and for George, Henry and Joseph

"... You need only to be still."

Contents

First Thoughts

"In addition to sharing a cosmological worldview with their neighbours, the Jewish scribes who compiled the Hebrew Scripture shared literary sensibilities with them. If, like me, you read the Epic of Gilgamesh in college, you already know there are striking similarities between that Akkadian poem, which likely pre-dates Genesis, and the story of Noah. Both involve a worldwide flood and a noble character who builds a boat, rescues the Earth's animals, releases birds to see if the waters have subsided, and eventually survives when the boat comes to rest on a mountain. Questions regarding which community borrowed from which are less important than simply acknowledging the fact that Israel shared a conceptual world with its neighbours and used similar literary genres and stories to address issues of identity and purpose."

(Held Evans,2018)

This quote, from the late Rachel Held Evans, in her book "Inspired", serves to remind me that stories have a voice which can speak to us no matter where they are found. The immersion in and the gradual reflection on the story are so much more important than its origin. This is because it has always been more important for us to use a story to help to form our own worldview than it is to merely "know about" an old story whether it be from holy text or folklore. Far more powerful is our ability to learn from an old story and apply this understanding in our own lives. Stories help us to make sense of things in the here and now.

My work in writing this book has been driven by my passion to bring reflective and immersive storytelling into classroom R.E. across all Key Stages. This method creates space for awe and wonder and champions the recommendations of Mary Myatt (marymyatt.com 8 June 2020) as it privileges thinking over task completion, encourages time for mastery and uses materials which are beautiful. Our children deserve great experiential learning and, as our brains privilege story, treating it in a different way to other information, it seems an obvious and powerful tool to utilise. Research shows that facts are more than 20 times more likely to be remembered if delivered as part of a story. What better way to deliver information?

Although, as a practitioner, you may want your pupils to know about the origin and background of the story you tell, can I strongly invite you to use verbal wondering, which I will explain in more detail in a while. At the end of the sharing of each story, verbal wondering is a chance to provide the opportunity for pupils to question motivation and purpose of the characters, settings and action and to apply wisdom from these texts into their life experiences. As ever in R.E. it is as important to learn from religion and non-religious worldviews as it is to learn about them.

The Journey

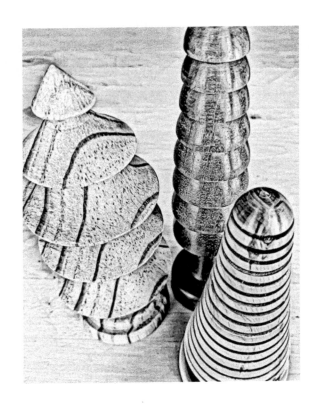

"without hesitation, the woodcutter strode up to the tallest tree and chopped it down …"

I can still recall that moment, my shock, the feeling of the carpet on my leg, the intimacy, the wonder. That was the beginning of my journey into reflective storytelling, a huge marker on the path of my becoming and the conception of Time To Wonder. I was 46 years old, sat on the floor in a room in Wells, Somerset watching a lady I didn't know, tell a story I had never heard, using a method I had never seen. But I was beguiled, this was something special. I knew at that moment that this way of delivering story had such power and that it needed to be shared. This was not "telling", this was "sharing", it was about community and connection but it was also deeply personal and a mindful way of wondering. This was not just for children and it wasn't limited to Christian tradition. This method of storytelling was for everyone. I had to learn more.

So, I decided to take a look at the storytelling method known as Godly Play, because this would provide me with framework with which I could begin to develop my own practice. The storytelling I had seen in Wells had been introduced as Godly Play and although its essence was not a million miles away, as I found out, Godly Play was something rather different.

Godly Play is a storytelling method with its roots in Montessori teaching. Godly Play was developed in the USA over several decades by a church leader called Jerome Berryman who had a particular interest in the theology of childhood. His intention was to use the method within churches to help develop children's spirituality and religious language.

I knew I wanted to develop a method to fit school settings and to encompass stories from other religions in order to support the provision of the teaching of Religion and Worldviews. I decided to create something new, with echoes of Godly Play within it, but suitable for the purpose of delivering stories in RE and use elsewhere too. After careful thought I decided on a new title, Time to Wonder Reflective Storytelling.

Being in the Story

I wonder if you have ever been whisked away into another place through story? Most of us, if we enjoy reading, will know that marvellous feeling. It is almost an essential quality of a good book, the ability to transport us away from the familiar and place us into somewhere new, somewhere *otherly.* In our minds we have the capacity to create the most incredible worlds, to evoke feelings and imagine characters. I believe these skills are innate, that is to say, we naturally have within us the capacity to transcend our reality and move into our imaginations and rest there.

I remember, one summer when my eldest son was only four or five years old, we went out into the garden one warm day and snuggled together on the wooden swing seat under a small tree. I began to read Roald Dahl's Danny, The Champion of The World and my young son sat, head cocked to one side, looking far out and up towards the whisps of cloud high above our heads. He was usually such a livewire, but this story utterly captivated him and he transcended his mortality and became lodged inside the book. So deep was his experience, that when I stopped reading and announced it was time for lunch, he took a moment or two to return to the swing seat. He looked at me sorrowfully; "Mum," he pleaded "please don't stop, I was in the story". This feeling is a powerful one, and we can also experience it through the media of music, poetry, film and other art forms. For thousands and thousands of years, human beings have been finding ways to share stories and there are increasingly diverse ways to achieve this end. The method I want to discuss and promote I believe to be an ancient one, reflective storytelling in the manner of Time to Wonder has the power to put us into the story and cradle us there.

Reflective Storytelling -
the Method and Points to Note

The method itself is not revolutionary, in some ways it's as old as the hills! Way before the relatively recent invention of film and television, before the printing press and the skill of reading written script, stories were shared orally and in community. Initially using art; like the 17,000 year old cave paintings still in evidence in Lascaux, France or the 30,000 year old ones in the Acacus Mountains in Libya, as well as several other sites across the globe, objects of human creation served to help to share story and embed it. So, in essence, the human condition is hard-wired for the Time To Wonder method of reflective storytelling. We have been hearing stories told this way since almost the very beginning of our existence on Earth.

I would argue that the method is rather countercultural too. In this way of storytelling, your community need to be stilled, present and reflective. So often nowadays we are asked to become busy, distracted and consumed by the need to produce something, create something, be something that others require. Reflective storytelling counters these current ideas, the method courageously, quietly and strongly rejects the notion that we need to be continually doing, instead it invites the community to simply be.

In basic terms, this is the pattern to follow as you use the reflective storytelling process:

a) A welcomed, comfortable Community
b) Getting Ready
c) Story Sharing
d) Wondering together
e) Continued response
f) Group reflection.

Each aspect is explained in more detail below, along with a few extra considerations. These are all important points to remember before it is possible to deliver a reflective story successfully.

Commitment

Initially, it is essential to understand that this method requires commitment to the entire process. In order for reflective storytelling to draw the community (those gathered to listen) into itself, the storyteller must be fully invested. More than that, the storyteller needs to be in the story themselves. So it is that the requirement is to position oneself comfortably, getting ready for the story and considering it before the community settle to listen. Alternatively, if the children are already in the room with you, which is most likely in school, take a moment after the community are settled and ready. Take a couple of breaths whilst you settle yourself and get ready in your own mind for the adventure ahead. The story must be given reverence, the community will be aware of the storyteller's energy and will only wonder deeply if the storyteller provides the environment to promote this. Some of the devices I use to assist in this include; removing jewellery from my hands, wrists and neck line, wearing plain coloured clothes, taking a couple of deep breaths before I begin, speaking in a calm, relaxed manner, maintaining my focus on the story, pausing if I feel the need, either for myself or for the community.

a) A Welcomed, Comfortable Community

The community must feel welcomed. In a classroom situation the children are likely to already be in the room where the story will take place, so the welcome can be developed through verbal cues from the storyteller, something like; "Welcome everyone, we are all gathered to hear a story, I wonder if you are ready to listen?"

As well as verbal cues, the physical provision of space to accommodate everyone and a relaxed and comfortable atmosphere are really important. The community should sit in a circle which includes space for the storyteller and you might like them to remove their shoes. These are cues about this time being different to the rest of the day. The circle can be on the floor or on chairs, or you might choose to gather around a table. You know your setting and your community and will make your own judgments about the most comfortable, welcoming and inclusive scenario.

b) Getting Ready

The storyteller needs to prepare the community for the process, particularly in cases where they have not seen a story delivered in this way before. Often, for those who haven't experienced a reflective story before, the slow pace and the silence can be a little daunting. I'd really encourage a brief explanation of what the community should expect; the process of storying together, the need to watch the story happen in space in front of the storyteller, that the storyteller will be looking at the story too, not at the community, and that there will be time for verbal wondering together afterwards. It's especially important to stress that individuals should not feel the need to speak if they don't wish to during the verbal wondering. I always say that there is much which will be said, but just as much will be unsaid. The unsaid will be just as important. You may wish to talk a little about the process of wondering, about how it is a chance for our minds to wander around a subject, story or idea, that there will be lots of thoughts and all of them are important and valuable, but also to say that this is a time to simply be, to enjoy the story time, to relax. This will help to support anyone feeling anxious about it. You will know the children you are working with very well, if you feel they need a short time to ask questions about the process before you begin, then use the getting ready as that opportunity.

Finally, the community need to take a moment to settle themselves. If they have already experienced reflective storytelling then they will know what is coming and will often be settling themselves without prompting. The settling time is a time for stilling or mindfulness practice and can also be a time for the use of a prayer. When telling a story from Buddhism, Hinduism or Sikhism you might welcome everyone with "Namaste" or use "Assalamu Alaykum" with a story from Islam. Body prayers* or short verses from holy text might be employed. There is nothing which is set, apart from a short time in which to shrug off what has gone before and be ready, in the moment, for the story to come.
I usually say something like;

"If we are really going to be able to enjoy this story time, we need to be ready. You can get ready in many ways, you can make your body still and quiet, you can take a few deep breaths, you can notice how you are feeling. When I am telling the story, I won't be looking at you and I won't be answering any questions you might have. To really enjoy the story, you will need to look at the space in front of me where the story will take place. After the story is finished, I will adjust my body position and look up. At that point I will ask a question beginning with the words "I Wonder" and that will be the time when we can begin to wonder about the story altogether. This will be a time to talk about what we liked, what was important, how it made us feel, but if you don't want to say anything, that's ok too, it doesn't mean you're not wondering."

A prayer using body parts, examples can easily be found online.

Suitable space

The more I use the Time to Wonder reflective storytelling technique, the more I realise that its power transcends many obstacles, particularly in the school environment.

I appreciate a warm, cosy, carpeted room away from the hustle and bustle of the rest of school life, but it is extremely unusual to be gifted such a space. Usually, Time to Wonder takes place in the midst of a busy classroom where a teacher might be sat at their desk marking English books while I tell the story with my back to the interactive board kneeling next to a box of lost property.

What I have learned is that if my intention is wholehearted and I have the right materials, I'm confident in the story and the community is settled and comfortable, then we can still fully engage in the process. You will need to ensure enough space for the entire community to settle comfortably. This might mean removing shoes and sitting in a circle on the floor, or it could be sitting in chairs around a table. I have told stories one to one across a low coffee table and to a group of 40 seated on chairs in concentric rings. Whilst small groups tend to generate the best responses. I would not rule anything out. In classrooms, the most important thing you can provide in terms of space is to ensure you are not sat with your back to the door. This will hopefully mean that the focus remains on the story and storyteller even if someone enters or leaves the room (other staff members perhaps).

c) Story Sharing

That feeling of immersion, to have felt held by the story and left wanting more. This is how we must approach the work of reflective storytelling, with commitment to invest in the process sufficiently that our audience experience those same feelings. Not only this, but we must ensure that we remain the conduit for the story and not the focus of the community's attention. To this end we must avoid using facial expression or our hands in ways which could detract from the materials as the story unfolds before us. For this reason, it is important not to look at the audience and to remain focussed on the materials throughout the storytelling. In this way, the audience are constantly drawn back into the story and away from the teller. It is also important to learn the script. This may sound obvious, but without fully knowing the story you cannot possibly provide that immersive experience. In this instance, the idea of "knowing" means you have studied the story in sufficient detail that you are familiar with it to the degree that you are confidently able to see the twists and turns of it in your mind's eye. Your audience don't know the script word for word! It is more important to know the story than to churn out the script by rote. The emotions and the actions will carry you through the story.

This takes some time, energy and practise before you can truly feel at ease. But I have tried to make the scripts as user friendly as possible; I'm aware of the many demands on the average class teacher and am trying to support you with a useful tool. When I am learning a new story, initially I read the script alongside my materials and move the materials whilst I am reading from the script. In this way I find the materials cue my next sentence, or if not, at least jog my memory about which part of the story comes next. After all, it is the materials which help the listener to embed the story far better in their own minds, so it follows that the materials will provide the storyteller with the right cues and support their memory too.

Finally, I remove the written script and tell the story without it. At first it can be challenging, but fairly quickly you will settle into the tempo, words and phrases and feel far more at ease. One of the beautiful things about reflective storytelling is the pace; slow and measured. This can be a huge advantage in the spilt second when you forget the next line of the script, it gives you a chance to regain that which was lost.

Just remember; **don't look up or use wondering questions until the story is complete.**

Very occasionally you may have a listener who becomes distracted and subsequently is distracting for others. Do NOT look up. Simply stop storytelling, place your hands in your lap. You might want to say something like; "It seems we are not all ready. I will wait until everyone is ready once more…" You won't need any more of a cue than that. Mostly, even the simple act of stopping will be enough for the distraction to end. Low level quiet comments and shared observations between community members should not count as enough distraction to need to stop. Often these are worth capturing and remembering as they may fuel the verbal wondering later. In some instances, they may also inform assessment.

Once the story is finished, be aware that the putting away is just as important. This happens once the verbal wondering time has finished; during the verbal wondering, the story will aid as a cue for some of the thinking and speaking. Sand should be brushed carefully from each piece, items placed back into their basket or box slowly and with reverence. The story is not finished until the materials look just as they did before it began.

Appropriate materials

Whilst I have endeavoured to keep the amount of materials required to a minimum, those used should be considered carefully and chosen to reflect the sacred nature of the story being told. Never forget that the story you are sharing is an extremely important one to many millions of people and should always be treated with reverence. The way you handle the materials and your overall demeanour speak volumes well before you use any words.

Think about the materials you choose to use. They are as much a part of the story as the words you will weave and the actions you will attach to them. These materials must infer the importance of the story for millions of people around the world. For this reason, it is crucial to choose wisely. The materials need to be robust as they will be used over and over, not just by the storyteller, but also by those who hear the story and choose to subsequently utilise the materials during their continued response time.

Also, it can be useful to make links between the comparative religions of Christianity, Islam and Judaism in the materials. I use sand and wood to tell Torah stories of Abraham and Moses, stories from the life of Jesus from the New Testament and also for stories from Islam. This is unspoken, but it references the links between these religions and the geography and historical context they spring from. When telling stories from Buddhism, Hinduism or Sikhism the materials look very different to reflect the differences of culture and geography. Sand is replaced with brightly coloured silks and satins and the plain wooden figures and simple wooden blocks are gone. In their stead, the figures are ornately decorated with bright colours, gold and silver. This reflects the opulence and decorations associated with the Asia Pacific region.

Handling and sourcing the materials

Great care should be taken when handling the materials, which makes unspoken reference to the precious and sacred quality of the story. Gently remove each piece from the basket or box you take it from, carefully placing it onto the sand or cloth. Each time you move the pieces, do so slowly and with care. Ensure you pick up the people and animals with special care, not by their heads!

There are a few excellent suppliers for materials, these are listed at the end of the book. Much of the storytelling materials I have sourced or produced myself. Teachers are notoriously good at hoarding treasures from charity shops, garage sales and the like and I'd really encourage you to be on the look out for items you can save for storytelling. I would, whatever materials you decide to use, suggest that these materials are kept separate from the other classroom supplies. In order to retain the "otherly" nature of Time To Wonder reflective storytelling and to ensure the sacred character of the materials remains, it is important to use materials which don't simply get amalgamated into the other classroom kit.

d) Wondering together

In this section of the process, teacher agency can make a big impact. The key here is to use open questions and start them with "I wonder..." and to be ready to wait in silence. If no-one responds verbally, that doesn't mean there is no wondering going on.

It is important for the teacher to steer, but not control rigidly, the verbal response session, but at the same time remain impartial in a similar way to when facilitating P4C or other debates. Try to respond to anything which is said in an earnest way. The children need to know that any answer they give will not be judged harshly. They must feel safe if they are willing to risk trying to say things which may be difficult to express or hard to explain.

During 2018 an interesting research project was undertaken by Georgina Uttley, a student at the University of Huddersfield, UK (Is Godly Play good for RE? Uttley, 2018). The focus was on the Godly Play method and its effectiveness as a tool for delivering parts of the RE curriculum. Its findings were not unexpected. In essence, the findings suggested the need to move away from the limited list of questions suggested in pure Godly Play and move towards questioning which is still open and full of wondering, but could be driven by your assessment aims.

If you are telling the story of The Night of Power from Islam you may want to ask questions about the Prophet's emotions and experience for example, or you may wish to concentrate on understanding that this story explains the origins of the Qur'an and shows Prophet Muhammad (pbuh) in submission to the will of Allah.

I often find the addition of the question "I wonder if there's something you'd like to talk about that we haven't mentioned yet? " opens up a whole new strand of dialogue and often gives authority for the wondering to expand beyond the expected. Likewise, if you have little time for verbal wondering it can be closed down quite swiftly. Remember that this group activity is an important part of the process though, so allocate at least 10 minutes to it.

You may wish to record the verbal responses either using audio or written methods. If you have another adult in the room, they can scribe for you during this time. It is important that you don't stop and start the wondering whilst you make notes as this will affect the community. You need to keep your full attention on responses, the silences and the flow during this part of the session.

Be very clear, throughout the wondering, that you are comfortable with times of silence. This is really important because otherwise the community may feel it necessary to fill the silence simply to please. The value of the wondering time is in the opportunity simply to be; not having to speak if it doesn't feel necessary and to be comfortable to do so. At the end of the wondering you might say something like "Is there anything we have left out?" and then "As we finish our wondering together, we are grateful for all of the wonderings, those which we have heard and those which have remained silent".

e) Continued Response

This is the point at which the community have the opportunity to continue to respond to the story in whichever way they chose. This could be time for quiet contemplation, drawing, painting, play doh or other artistic responses, listening to music, reading, using a labyrinth, building blocks, drama and so on. In a classroom setting and with the constraints of our curriculum however, it is a time where the teacher can, once again, direct the response in order to deliver a more easily assessable outcome. It is still possible to use any or all of the suggested ideas, but with increased agency. Within your lesson plan, you will have an assessment goal in mind and along with the verbal response time, the continued response opportunity can help to realise these goals.

Remain alert but also keep a respectful distance during the period of continued response, particularly if you have given a creative free rein to the time allocated. Stories can whip up powerful emotions and some children may not be able to fully express themselves if they feel their work is going to be monitored or marked or they will need to justify their creations. It is important to expressly mention that work will not be marked or discussed in this case.

The other important consideration for Continued Response is the time you are able to allocate to it. If you can, you should give the community at least 30 minutes for their response. If you do this, you are placing value on this time which means the community will too. If you only have 10 minutes until the end of the lesson, don't offer any continued response, otherwise you will infer that it's really not that important a task and doesn't deserve to be given any time. A rushed experience would be in stark contrast to the rest of the reflective storytelling process and should be avoided.

On occasion, if time is limited, I have given everyone a piece of playdough whilst they remained in the storytelling circle and asked them to wonder with it for 5 or 10 minutes. This is an open invitation to just hold the dough, fiddle with it or create something more artistic. Because it is time limited though, it is unlikely to be as creative a response.

f) Group reflection

At the end of each session, it is important to offer a few moments of reflection. The community has spent time focussed on work which they will now need to leave as they prepare to return to the usual rhythm of the setting. This is not a time for "show and tell", although some children may want to share the individual work they have created. It is important that it is made clear at the end of the time of shared verbal wondering that there will not be any pressure to share the individual responses created subsequently, because sometimes stories can trigger powerful feelings for members of the listening community. Conversely, you need to be prepared to respond appropriately if someone does choose to share something personal.

Story Scripts

In this book I have detailed a few of the scripts I have used for core teaching in primary and secondary settings. It is my intention that subsequent publications will increase the breadth of the scripted stories available. So, if you love these scripts, consider them a taster of things to come!

Each script is prefaced by the detail of where the original story can be found, some history about its origin and some information about the main characters. I am acutely aware, particularly in the primary sector, that many teachers are delivering RE without much, if any, RE specific training and with little time or resources at their disposal. Therefore, apart from gathering the materials, I want this resource to be everything you need in order to understand the process, deliver the story and guide the verbal wondering. The continued responses will be tailored by each teacher to afford the best opportunities for assessment, but I would suggest ensuring the children have options at this point in order to continue the feeling of the whole experience being a journey of wonder.

The scripts are ones I use most often throughout KS1 and KS2. These stories are also suitable for KS3 and KS4 and I would very much encourage the use of reflective storytelling in secondary settings. In my experience, stories are received extremely positively by secondary learners. Of course, where you choose to dive in is up to you, your locally agreed syllabus or teaching point will dictate a particular story. Don't be afraid to tell a story more than once to the same cohort, particularly at the beginning and end of a scheme of work. Also, delivering the same story at different Key Stages can be very fruitful...what someone wonders when they hear a reflective story as a 5-year-old is likely to be entirely different to their wondering at Upper KS2 or in KS3.

Index of Story Scripts

The Blind Men
and The Elephant

Preface

This is a story which the Lord Siddhartha told and it can be found in The Udana from the Pali Canon. This text can also be found in Hindu and Jain texts and it is impossible to know its precise origins. The Buddha explained that the reason for telling the story was that "Some (people) are deeply attached to their own views; people who only see one side of things engage in quarrels and disputes". The story illustrates **the many sidedness of all things and challenges individual perspective.**

You will need:

- **A box or basket to hold the following items:**
- **A cloth to denote the land, perhaps green or brown silk**
- **An elephant statue**
- **A few building blocks to build a little wall with**
- **A snake**
- **A spear**
- **A cow, much smaller than the elephant, I use a picture of one**
- **A fan**
- **A piece of frayed rope.**

Speech is shown in standard font with instructions in **bold.**

Story

Before you begin, ensure the children are ready. You might encourage them to take some deep breaths altogether in order to be settled and present. Once you begin to tell the story keep your focus on the story and don't look up until you have finished.

Lay down the cloth in front of you with purpose and intention. Ensure it is smoothed and then take a moment before you begin to speak;

Long ago six old men lived in a village in India. Each one had been born blind. Since the blind men could not see the world for themselves, they had to imagine many of its wonders. The men were curious about many things in life, but they were most curious about elephants

Place the elephant in the centre of the cloth.

They were told that elephants could trample forests, carry huge loads, and frighten people with their loud trumpet calls. But they also knew that the King's daughter rode an elephant when she travelled around the kingdom. Would the King let his daughter get near such a dangerous creature?

So it was, one day, the blind men were invited to touch an elephant. In this way they would finally discover what it they were really like.

The first blind man reached out and touched the side of the huge animal. "An elephant is smooth and solid like a wall!" he declared. "It must be very powerful."

With the building blocks, build a wall between you and the elephant. You're going to place each subsequent item in a circle equidistant from the elephant, so consider the wall's distance from the elephant in order to fit everything in.

The second blind man put his hand on the elephant's trunk. "An elephant is like a giant snake," he announced.

Place the snake close to the elephant's trunk.

The third blind man felt the elephant's pointed tusk. "I was right," he decided. "This creature is as sharp and deadly as a spear."

Place the spear close to the snake and the elephant's tusk.

The fourth blind man touched one of the elephant's four legs. "What we have here," he said, "is an extremely large cow."

Place the cow close to one of the elephant's legs.

The fifth blind man felt the elephant's giant ear. "I believe an elephant is like a huge fan to provide cool air in the heat of the day" he said.

Place the fan close to the elephant's ear.

The sixth blind man gave a tug on the elephant's coarse tail. "Why, this is nothing more than a piece of old rope. Dangerous, indeed," he scoffed.

Place the rope close to the elephant's tail.

They were unable to agree on what an elephant was really like;

"Wall!" "Snake!" "Spear!" "Cow!" "Fan!" "Rope!"

Adjust your posture and look up from the story before continuing. Don't forget to allow plenty of silence in between questions if there are no verbal responses. Wondering happens in silence as often as it does out loud!

I wonder *(suggestions ...)*

- Which part of this story you like the best?
- Which part of the story you think is most important?
- If any of the blind men were right about the elephant? Were any of them completely wrong?
- How it feels when another person doesn't "see" something the way you do?

Once the verbal wondering is complete it is time to put the story away. Make sure you do this slowly and with intention, in the same way that you initially laid it out. Ask the community to quieten whilst you do this and you may like to remind them, with words, of the pieces you're putting away as you go. For example;

Here is the elephant who was so many different things.

Now it is time for the Individual continued Response or an assessment task.

If you decide to allow the community a choice of response media, explain that at this point and then release them one by one from the storytelling circle as they have chosen which medium they will work with. Remind them that the IR time is a quiet and reflective continuation of what has gone before. They should continue to consider the story and their response to it.

The Forgiving Father

Preface

A New Testament Bible story found in the gospel of Luke (15: 11-32) with many themes to mine including: **stories Jesus told, monotheism, relationship with God, equity, agape love, redemption, forgiveness, greed and loss.** This is a response to the Pharisee who complain that Jesus spends time with "undesirables". Jesus explains God's love for those who are "lost" and subsequently "found".

You will need:

- **A sand bag (sand in a large cloth bag which can be opened out flat)**
- **A small container to hold the figures, coins, goblet and pig**
- **Three wooden figures (the old man and his two sons)**
- **A couple of coins**
- **A goblet**
- **A pig.**

Speech is shown in standard font with instructions in **bold.**

Story

Before you begin, ensure the children are ready. You might encourage them to take some deep breaths altogether in order to be settled and present. Once you begin to tell the story keep your focus on the story and don't look up until you have finished.

I wonder if you have ever lost something that is very precious to you and then just when you thought that it was lost forever, you found it again? Can you remember how you felt?

Place the sand bag in front of you and begin to open it and lay it flat. Now look down and still yourself for a moment before beginning to tell the story. Reflect on the scene before you launch into the spoken word. Don't look up again until you have finished.

Begin to run your hands through the sand making shapes and patterns in it as you say the following words.

This is an important place, every place holds stories from long ago. This story is very old, but it is still remembered today. Many Christians believe the stories Jesus told help people to understand what God is like. The stories Jesus told are precious to most Christians, and they are very old stories, but many Christians believe they are still important and have something to teach us.

Pause to clean the sand from your hands before saying;

There was an old man with two sons.

Place three wooden figures together onto the sand, furthest to your right, do this with care, don't handle the figures by their heads, treat each one respectfully as if human.

The eldest son

touch one of the figures

was hard-working and loyal, he was content with life on the farm. The younger son

touch another wooden figure

was restless and impatient and he found life on the farm rather dull. One day he told his father he had been thinking that if he could have his share of the father's fortune now instead of waiting until the old man died, he would be able to travel and see the world and have some fun before he got too old.

Although the old man

touch the remaining figure

knew he would be sad to see his son go, he agreed. He remembered when he was young how impatient he had been to know what the world was like.

And so, the son packed up and left.

Move the son to your left, a little way away from the old man and the other figure.

Time passed, days, weeks and months went by

pause, then touch the old man gently.

The old man missed his son. Meanwhile,

lay the coins and goblet onto the sand to the left of the figure of the younger son

the youngest son had spent all of his money on parties, he was poor. He needed to find work and a place to live. He ended up looking after some pigs and having to sleep with them in their sty.

Place the pig to the left of the coins and goblet. Move the youngest son to be next to the pigs.

He knew he had been foolish and had nothing to show for his time away. He decided he would return home and beg his father for forgiveness. He hoped he would be forgiven.

As you say the next few lines you need to, very slowly, move the youngest son back across the sand from left to right. Have him "stagger" and falter a few times.

He staggered slowly along, stumbling towards his home.

Make sure there is still a space between the youngest son and the father.

As he got closer to home the old man saw him in the distance. It was his youngest son. He had returned!

Now begin to move the figure of the old man towards the youngest son.

The old man ran to meet him. His son was so sorry for everything. The old man was so overjoyed that he didn't care about any of that.

Move both figures until they are back with the third, on the right-hand side of the felt.

Through tears of joy he called to his servants and asked them to prepare a great feast. His son had been lost and now he was found.

The eldest son complained when he found out what was happening.

Touch the eldest son

The youngest son had wasted all that had been given to him and instead of punishment, he was being rewarded with a great feast! The eldest son had worked hard and done what was right all his life and yet the father had never arranged a great feast for him!

Touch the figure of the old man

"You are both my sons and I love you both dearly," the old man explained.

"I thought that your brother had gone forever but now he is home. He was lost, but now he is found."

Adjust your posture and look up from the story before continuing. Don't forget to allow plenty of silence in between questions if there are no verbal responses. Wondering happens in silence as often as it does out loud!

I wonder *(suggestions ...)*

- Which part of this story you liked the best?
- How the eldest son felt when his brother left home?
- How the youngest son felt when he left home?
- How the father recognised his son, even when he was still far away?

Once the verbal wondering is complete it is time to put the story away. Make sure you do this slowly and with intention, in the same way that you initially laid it out. Ask the community to quieten whilst you do this and you may like to remind them, with words, of the pieces you're putting away as you go. For example;

"Here is the older brother who felt things were unfair."

Now it is time for the Continued Response or an assessment task.

If you decide to allow the community a choice of response media, explain that at this point and then release them one by one from the storytelling circle as they have chosen which medium they will work with. Remind them that the CR time is a quiet and reflective continuation of what has gone before. They should continue to consider the story and their response to it.

The Hidden Treasure

Preface

This story originates as a legend from the oral tradition of storytelling. It helps to introduce the concept of the many **avatars** within the Hindu religion. It also helps to explain the concept of **divinity in all things** and the origins of **"Namaste"**, which describes recognition of the spark of god or divinity in every living thing.

You will need:

- A box or basket (it should speak of the South Asian region in its design and colours)
- Two pieces of fabric to represent land and sea (browns or greens for the land and blues for the ocean). I have sewn mountain shapes onto my land silk in one spot and some wavy ribbons of blue silk onto the ocean to represent waves, but this is not essential
- A selection of figures to represent Hindu gods (I painted a selection of different sizes and shapes of wooden peg dolls in bright colours incorporating gold and silver paint, in this way the concept of many differing qualities of god and the many avatars Hindus revere is visible if unspoken)
- A heart which could be made of wood or you might choose to use stone, material, papier mache etc ...

Speech is shown in standard font with instructions in **bold.**

Story

Before you begin, ensure the children are ready. You might encourage them to take some deep breaths all together in order to be settled and present. Once you begin to tell the story keep your focus on the story and don't look up until you have finished.

Using pieces of silk of suitable colours create a storytelling landscape. Next, place a selection of the gods onto the land silk choosing as many differing sizes, shapes and colours as you can. Place them in a circle indicating a forum or meeting, do this with care, don't handle the figures by their heads, treat each one respectfully as if living. There should always be more gods in the box than you need.

Now look down and still yourself for a moment before beginning to tell the story. Reflect on the scene before you launch into the spoken word. Don't look up again until you have finished.

This is an important place, every place holds stories from long ago. According to an old Hindu legend, there was once a time when all human beings were gods, but they behaved badly, so badly that Brahma decided to take away their godliness or divinity and hide it where it could never be found.

But where to hide it?

Pause momentarily.

So, Brahma called a council of the gods to help him decide

use your hand to indicate the council circle.

"Let's bury it deep in the earth," said the council. But Brahma answered, "No, that will not do because humans will dig into the earth and find it."

Move the gods from their original circle to the ocean cloth, they should all be in the ocean before you say

Then the council said, "Let's sink it in the deepest part of the ocean." But Brahma said, "No, not there, for they will learn to dive into the ocean and will find it."

Move the gods from their ocean circle to the land cloth (on the mountains if you have some marked), they should all be in the mountains before you say

Then they said, "Let's take it to the top of the highest mountain and hide it there." But once again Brahma replied, "No, that will not do either, because they will eventually climb every mountain and once again take up their divinity."

move the gods from their postion in the mountains, back to the position of their original forum when the story began. Take your time.

Then the council gave up and said, "We do not know where to hide it, because it seems that there is no place on earth or in the sea that human beings will not eventually reach."

Brahma thought for a long time and then said, "Here is what we will do.

Take the heart out of the box and cradle it in your hand as you slowly show everyone in the circle how it is nestled into your palm...then say:

We will hide their divine power deep within their own being, humans will never think to look for it there." All the deities agreed that this was the perfect hiding place.

Place the wooden heart in the centre of the circle of gods.

Since then, humans have searched for their divinity, looking everywhere for something which is already deep within themselves.

Adjust your posture and look up from the story before continuing. Don't forget to allow plenty of silence in between questions if there are no verbal responses. Wondering happens in silence as often as it does out loud!

I wonder *(suggestions ...)*

- Which part of that story you thought was the most important part?
- If the hiding or the searching is the most important action?
- If you have ever searched for something, but not found it/and found it?
- How did that make you feel?
- What makes this story important or special?

Once the verbal wondering is complete it is time to put the story away. Make sure you do this slowly and with intention, in the same way that you initially laid it out. Ask the community to quieten whilst you do this and you may like to remind them, with words, of the pieces you're putting away as you go. For example;

"Here is the heart representing the place where Brahma decided to hide human divinity."

Now it is time for the Continued Response or an assessment task.

If you decide to allow the community a choice of response media, explain that at this point and then release them one by one from the storytelling circle as they have chosen which medium they will work with. Remind them that the CR time is a quiet and reflective continuation of what has gone before. They should continue to consider the story and their response to it.

The Night of Power

(The 1st Revelation of The Holy Qur'an)

Preface

This is an important story for most Muslims. It details when the Prophet Muhammad (pbuh) received the very first revelation of The Holy Qur'an. Muslims celebrate this during the month of Ramadan on the 23rd or 27th night. It is considered the highlight of Ramadan and the holiest night of the entire year. The Qur'an says that worshipping Allah on this night is more rewarding than doing so for 1000 months. Many Muslims spend the whole night praying or reciting the Qur'an.

Themes to highlight in this story are **submission, Iman (faith), revelation, angels, destiny, making positive impacts and respect and reverence for The Qur'an.**

You will need:

- **A sand bag (sand in a large cloth bag which can be opened out flat)**
- **A small container to hold the wooden block and the representation of the Prophet (pbuh)**
- **A wooden block to indicate the Ka'bah in the city of Mecca**
- **A polished stone, crystal or other item instead of a human form.** *There must be no representation of Muhammad (pbuh) or any of his close friends as a person. Most Muslims believe this practice could encourage idolatry and is considered offensive.*

Speech is shown in standard font with instructions in **bold.**

Story

Before you begin, ensure the children are ready. You might encourage them to take some deep breaths altogether in order to be settled and present. Once you begin to tell the story keep your focus on the story and don't look up until you have finished.

Place the sand bag in front of you and begin to open it and lay it flat. Then begin to run your hands through the sand, make shapes in the sand including a flat area furthest from you and to your right, and a raised, hilly area closest to you...as you do this, begin the dialogue.

This is an important place, every place holds stories from long ago. This story is very old, but it is still remembered today. This is the story of a most sacred, holy night for Muslims. This story takes place in the desert, so we have a little piece of the desert here to help us to tell this story.

By this time, you have piled one area of the sand up a little to represent Mount Hira. Now place the wooden block too. Hira is north east of Mecca, so place the block below Hira and to your right, towards the furthest edge of the desert bag from the storyteller.

In an important city in the desert, a city called Mecca, lived a merchant called Muhammad.

At this point, place the stone or other object you're using to depict Prophet Muhammad onto the sand next to Mecca, do this with care, treat it respectfully as if living.

It was hot in the city, so hot that Muhammad wanted to escape. It was noisy in the city too, so noisy that he wanted to find somewhere peaceful. The people worshipped many idols; statues they thought of as gods. They spent time decorating them. Muhammad believed in one God. He wanted to spend time with God alone.

So, Muhammad left his home and walked up into the mountains.

Now begin to slowly move your indicator from Mecca towards the hills, take your time and create a pattern of prints in the sand, like footprints to show the journey.

Eventually, Muhammad reached the Cave of Hira.

Place your indicator on top of the hill and use your hands to create a cave shape around it for a moment.

It was cool and dark. It was peaceful. Muhammad felt calm. He thought about God.

Move your hands away from your indicator and pause.

Suddenly, he realised he wasn't alone!

Use your hands locked together at the thumbs to create the angel before him.

There before him was a messenger from God, an angel, bathed in bright light. Muhammad was afraid! The angel Jibril gave him a written scroll and asked him to read it. Muhammad could not read. The angel asked again, Muhammad told the angel he could not read. For a third time, the angel asked Muhammad to read the scroll, in the name of the Lord who made all of creation. This time, Muhammad found he could read the words! It was as if the words had been written on his heart, the words were so important, he knew he would never forget them.

The hand angel can now disappear. Pause for a moment before you begin to move the indicator back towards Mecca.

Muhammad left the cave, still afraid and as he did, he heard a voice saying "Muhammad, you are God's messenger." He was wondering about all that had happened. What did it all mean? Muhammad told his wife, Khadijah, all about what had happened to him in the cave. The words were incredibly beautiful - but she knew immediately they were especially important too. She believed these were words from God and Muhammad, her husband, was God's messenger.

Adjust your posture and look up from the story before continuing. Don't forget to allow plenty of silence in between questions if there are no verbal responses. Wondering happens in silence as often as it does out loud!

I wonder *(suggestions ...)*

- Which is your favourite part of this story?
- Which part you think is the most important?
- How Prophet Muhammad felt when the angel appeared?
- How Prophet Muhammad felt when he told his wife Khadijah?
- Why Khadijah believed such an amazing story?
- If God can speak to people, even today? How?
- If you have a quiet place, somewhere you can go to think and be alone?

After the verbal wondering you may want to give the children the information below.

Over 23 years Prophet Muhammad received many more words from God. After Prophet Muhammad died, Abu Bakr and his scribes, who believed what he had said, wrote down all the words that Prophet Muhammad had been told by the angel Gabriel (Jibril), so that the words would never be forgotten. The book they wrote is called the Qur'an.

The word Qur'an means 'that which is read or recited'. Today the events of The 1st Revelation (Night of Power) are celebrated on the 23rd or 27th day of the month of Ramadan.

To most Muslims, the Qur'an is the most important book of all. They read and remember it; they take great care of it. They try to let it guide them in everything they do.

A final wondering question might be,

I wonder if you have a special book or a special person to guide you?

Once the verbal wondering is complete it is time to put the story away. Make sure you do this slowly and with intention, in the same way that you initially laid it out. Ask the community to quieten whilst you do this and you may like to remind them, with words, of the pieces you're putting away as you go. For example;

Here is Mecca, a city in the desert.

Now it is time for the Continued Response or an assessment task.
If you decide to allow the community a choice of response media, explain that at this point and then release them one by one from the storytelling circle as they have chosen which medium they will work with. Remind them that the CR time is a quiet and reflective continuation of what has gone before. They should continue to consider the story and their response to it.

Exodus - The Passover Story

Preface

The Passover of B'nai Israel, the Children of God, can be found in The Torah and the Old Testament in the book of Exodus. Adonai (God) was with the people as they "went out" (this is the literal meaning of the word "exodus") from slavery into freedom through the water. B'nai Israel look back on this time to sustain them when God is hidden and they feel lost. For most Jewish people Pesach (the Passover) keeps this story alive and the covenant between God and Moses is remembered every year. For most Jewish families, the Seder meal is a time for getting together to focus on the story, talk and eat special food. The Seder plate contains foods which remind the Jewish people when B'nai Israel were enslaved by the Egyptians and each food is highly symbolic.

This story explores many themes including: **covenant (relationship between God and the Jewish people), belonging, omnipotence, seeking refuge, persecution, liberation and redemption.**

You will need:

- **A sand bag (sand in a large cloth bag which can be opened out flat)**
- **A small container to hold the wooden figures and the blue strips of cloth**
- **Some small wooden figures to represent Moses, his brother Aaron and B'nai Israel, the Children of God**
- **Two narrow strips of blue cloth which can fit across the sand and overlap in the middle to form the Red Sea, parting and overlapping during the story**
- **A bowl of broken matzo.**

Speech is shown in standard font with instructions in **bold.**

Story

This story is an important one for most Jewish people. It is remembered every year during the festival of Pesach which is a Hebrew word meaning Passover. Sometimes during this story, you might notice me using words from the Hebrew language. It is a language many Jewish people use. Lots of Jewish children are taught Hebrew during Saturday School at their synagogue. The Jewish' holy text, the Torah scroll, is written in Hebrew. In this story you will hear me use the Hebrew word Adonai, which means God.

Before you begin, ensure the children are ready. You might encourage them to take some deep breaths altogether in order to be settled and present. Place the sand bag in front of you and begin to open it and lay it flat. Once you begin to tell the story keep your focus on the story and don't look up until you have finished. Start to run your hands through the sand, making hills and valleys, moving the sand from place to place…and begin the dialogue.

This is an important place, every place holds stories from long ago. This story is very old, but it is still remembered today. So many important things happened in this place to B'nai Israel, the Children of God.

As you finish speaking, clean your hands carefully to remove the residue of sand. Do this slowly and mindfully. Begin to place Moses and the other figures onto the desert sand in a group to your right and furthest from you (geographically correct as a viewer, this area would be Egypt) Do this with care, don't handle the figures by their heads, treat each one respectfully as if living.

B'nai Israel were living in a place called Egypt. In the land of Egypt, the leader was called Pharaoh. B'nai Israel had to do everything Pharaoh said. Whatever Pharaoh wanted, B'nai Israel did; they built for him, they farmed for him, they worked for him. Pharaoh did not pay them to do all this work, B'nai Israel were enslaved, they were trapped by Pharaoh and the people of Egypt.

Use both of your hands to create a cage around the wooden figures, pause for a moment once the cage is in place before moving the figures of Moshe/ Moses and Aaron away from the rest of the figures and a little closer to you

Adonai spoke to Moshe or Moses and told him to talk to Pharaoh. Moshe and his brother Aaron, went to Pharaoh and said, "Adonai, our God, says "Let my people go."

Pause

Pharaoh said, "No."

As you say this word, use your hand to form a flat palm and thrust it towards the figures of Moses and Aaron. Walk Moses and Aaron back to the original group. Pause, and then walk Moses and Aaron back towards Pharaoh

Moshe and Aaron went back many times to tell Pharaoh to let Adonai's people go, but Pharaoh always said, "No."

Thrust your palm forward again.

Then something terrible happened. The oldest boy in each Egyptian family died. Even Pharaoh's eldest son died. But B'nai Israel's sons did not die, because the people made a mark on the doors of their houses. They put the blood of a lamb there, and Adonai knew to pass over them. They were safe.

As you mention the passing over, use your hand to flow above the figures as if it were a wind or bird in flight, rising, passing over and then falling again.

When Moshe/Moses and Aaron went back this time and said, "Adonai, our God says, "Let my people go," Pharaoh said, "Yes."

This time, Pharaoh's response is less aggressive, imagine he is a broken man at the loss of his son. Instead of a flat palm, slowly offer a gently clenched fist without any power. Move Moses and Aaron back amongst the other figures.

The people packed all they could carry, and they baked bread for the journey.

There was no time to let the bread rise, it was flat. You can still eat this kind of bread, it is called matzo

Show the bowl of matzo.

Most Jewish people still eat matzo today when they celebrate this story at Pesach/Passover

place the bowl beside the sand.

The people went as quickly as they could

lay the blue felt across the sand in the centre stretching from the furthest point to the nearest to you so that they bisect the sand. Ensure the pieces overlap in the centre. Then begin to move the figures towards the blue felt, do this with some pace if possible.

They were afraid that Pharaoh would change his mind. Suddenly they heard a terrifying sound. The ground began to shake. Pharaoh's army was coming after them

by this time all the figures should be huddled next to the blue felt near to the overlap. Use your right hand to make a sweeping motion, holding your right hand vertically slowly move it from the far right in towards the figures as if the mighty army were closing in on B'nai Israel.

The thundering horses' hooves and the rolling of more than 600 chariots sounded very frightening! They did not know what to do.

Cup your hands directly over the figure of Moses

Adonai spoke to Moshe/Moses and Moshe knew what he should do.

Form a fist with your right hand, raise it up and then with force, hit the sandbag immediately adjacent to the sand. Then roll each strip of felt back to form a pathway through for the figures

He raised his staff and struck it against the ground and as he did, the waters parted to make a way for the people.

Begin to walk the figures through the pathway and try to animate them individually. One might travel at speed, whilst another might dance or yet another travel more slowly, until they are all on the other side of the felt. Your movements of the people indicate how they might feel; excited, afraid, nervous etc.

When all of B'nai Israel were safely on the other side, the water closed behind them

close the felt back down and overlap it once more

and they were free! Pharaoh could not reach them.

Adjust your posture and look up from the story before continuing.

This is like the flat bread the people made so quickly. You can still eat it today. Whenever you taste this bread, you taste the story. This is the bread of the Passover Feast. It is called "matzo." I am going to pass it around. I wonder if you would like to taste it? Every one of you may have a piece, but please don't take a piece if you don't want to. We will wait to taste it until everyone who wants to, has some.

Once everyone has had a chance to taste the matzo, continue with the wondering questions. Don't forget to allow plenty of silence in between questions if there are no verbal responses. Wondering happens in silence as often as it does out loud!

I wonder *(suggestions ...)*

- Which part of this story you like best?
- Which part of the story is the most important?
- If Moshe/Moses was afraid in this story? When? Why?
- What this story can tell us about what many Jewish people think God is like?
- What this story has to say about taking refuge/persecution/slavery etc ... (you will know if your class are ready for a question like this)?

Once the verbal wondering is complete it is time to put the story away. Make sure you do this slowly and with intention, in the same way that you initially laid it out. Ask the community to quieten whilst you do this and you may like to remind them with words of the pieces you're putting away as you go. For example;

This is the Red Sea that Adonai parted to give B'nai Israel a way to escape from Pharaoh.

Now it is time for Continued Response or an assessment task. If you decide to allow the community a choice of response media, explain that at this point and then release them one by one from the storytelling circle as they have chosen which medium they will work with. Remind them that CR time is a quiet and reflective continuation of what has gone before. They should continue to consider the story and their response to it.

The Kite

Preface

This is a folk story which has an unknown origin. It links well to **Humanist** themes about the **importance of supportive relationships, guidance and life lessons.**

You will need:

- **A sand bag (sand in a large cloth bag which can be opened out flat)**
- **A small container to hold the figures and kite**
- **Two wooden figures**
- **A (to scale) kite with a string tail (I use a homemade paper and PVA one and replace it if it gets damaged).**

Speech is shown in standard font with instructions in **bold.**

Story

Before you begin, ensure the children are ready. You might encourage them to take some deep breaths altogether in order to be settled and present.

Now look down and still yourself for a moment before beginning to tell the story. Once you begin to tell the story keep your focus on the story and don't look up until you have finished.

Take the sand bag and open it out in front of you with care. Once the bag is fully opened begin to shape the sand with your hand. As you move your hand in the sand you say:

This is an important place, every place holds stories from long ago.

Pause,

One day a father and his son went to fly a kite near to their house

place the two wooden figures onto the sand beside each other, do this with care, don't handle the figures by their heads, treat each one respectfully as if human.

The young boy had never flown a kite before and he was very excited to see just how high it would go

as you say this sentence take the kite from the small container, tuck one end of the string under the base of one of the figures. Float it just above the heads of the wooden figures and then slowly begin to raise it higher until the string becomes taut.

After a while, the son noticed it seemed that the kite string was stopping the kite from flying higher. "If we cut the string, the kite will be free and will go flying even higher", he said "Can we cut it?" So, the father cut the kite's string

use your fingers to create scissors and then make a cutting action on the string.

The kite started to fly a little higher

free the string from under the figure, move the kite upwards a little.

The boy was delighted.

But then, slowly, the kite started to come down

don't be too quick with this action, gradually float the kite down towards the ground, it can land a distance away from the two wooden figures.

It landed some distance from them. The young boy watched it fall. He had cut the kite loose so it could fly higher, but instead, it had fallen down.

Adjust your posture and look up from the story before continuing. Don't forget to allow plenty of silence in between questions if there are no verbal responses. Wondering happens in silence as often as it does out loud!

I wonder *(suggestions ...)*

- Which part of this story you liked the best?
- Which is the most important part of the story?
- How the boy felt as the kite fell to the ground?
- What the kite could really be?

Once the verbal wondering is complete it is time to put the story away. Make sure you do this slowly and with intention, in the same way that you initially laid it out. Ask the community to quieten whilst you do this and you may like to remind them, with words, of the pieces you're putting away as you go. For example;

"Here is the boy who wanted to set the kite free."

Now it is time for the Continued Response or an assessment task.

If you decide to allow the community a choice of response media, explain that at this point and then release them one by one from the storytelling circle as they have chosen which medium they will work with. Remind them that the CR time is a quiet and reflective continuation of what has gone before. They should continue to consider the story and their response to it.

Using Precious Artefacts

Storytelling is a natural extension to the revelation and exploration of artefacts during RE lessons. I would really encourage the same community approach to this activity and plenty of wondering to open up the minds of the children to what these artefacts might be saying about their owner, the religious tradition or community they come from and what can be learned about them and from them.

An artefact is something made for use in religion and also other worldviews, it should be something which is in use today, not a museum piece. It offers an enticing window into a religion or worldview. It may:

- Be used in worship (e.g. a chalice);
- Be a focus for reflection (e.g. an icon);
- Be a witness to others (e.g. a kippah);
- Express praise, gratitude or remembrance (an item which is a reminder of someone who was precious; a necklace, a pair of shoes, a scarf, a toy).

Religions and the non-religious use artefacts as reminders or prompts. Teachers can use artefacts to engage pupils in a process of discovery, to encourage them to think about the symbolism & not fix attention only on the outward object. Artefacts must not be merely shown, copied or described. As objects they are dumb, as artefacts, aiding understanding, they speak.

An artefact needs to be filled with meaning; with facts, stories, discussion, looking at the symbolism, the craftsmanship, how it is used, & the feelings of those who use it. We should not focus only on the externals of the artefact and its use but must ask questions like:

I wonder *(suggestions ...)*

- What does this mean to the owner/ user/ believer?
- How might it change their life?
- What beliefs or concepts does this artefact point to?
- How is this artefact relevant to me or my life?

Ideas for useful artefacts might include:

Buddhism

- Prayer beads – prayer
- Singing bowl and stick – meditation
- Votive stupa – veneration of Buddhist saints
- Statue of The Buddha – worship, respect, offerings.

Christianity

- A cross – Easter, agape love
- Candles – prayer focus, Jesus "Light of the World"
- Icons (images of Jesus) – denominations, reverence
- Rosary Beads – penance, prayer.

Hinduism

- Puja Tray – worship, the shrine
- Murtis – expressions of one God with many, divine qualities and attributes.

Islam

- Qur'an – unique revelation, unbroken tradition
- Prayer mat and compass – spiritual orientation and belonging, Ummah.

Judaism

- Passover (Seder) Plate – connection with history, slavery and freedom
- Torah Scroll and Yad (pointer) – specialness, covenant.

Non-religious

- A photograph – tradition, family
- A diary or other precious book, perhaps poetry – human accomplishment
- An artwork – human creativity
- Some other treasure; perhaps a piece of jewellery owned by a friend or relative who has died – memories from existence.

Suppliers

I have found these suppliers to be very useful.

St. Michael's Workshop, Bowthorpe Community Trust make wooden people, blocks and felt strips. They supply lots more too and have a good online presence.

https://shop.stmichaelsworkshop.com

The Ark Man, Gail and Barry Hooper are based in Somerset. They make beautiful wooden arks and I have commissioned many fabulous items from them. Get in touch with them if you want something special.

https://www.thearkman.co.uk

If you want to make your own sand bag, here are some instructions:

https://www.godlyplay.uk/wp-content/uploads/2013/05/Desert-bag-instructions.pdf

Finally, do get in touch if you need more advice about what you need and where to find it.

thetime2wonder@gmail.com

References

I have referenced the sources of inspiration for all of the stories where there is a clear singular source. Sometimes my source of inspiration is not the first, most original documented story; for example, where my inspiration is a Godly Play script, this has obviously taken source material from The Bible.

Dedication	The Bible Exodus 14:14
Held Evans, R (2018)	Inspired: Slaying Giants, Walking on Water, and Loving the Bible Again
The Blind Men and The Elephant	Udana 6.4, although this is unlikely to be the original source. Probably oral tradition originally.
The Forgiving Father	The Bible Luke 15:11-32
The Hidden Treasure	Original source unknown
The Night of Power	The Holy Qur'an Surah 97
Exodus	The Bible Exodus 3:7-14:31 Exodus, Godly Play script (Berryman, J W, The Complete Guide to Godly Play Volume 2:14 Presentations for Fall (2002), p. 65-72.)
The Kite	Original source unknown.

Acknowledgements

Throughout this book, I hope I have made it very clear to credit others honestly whenever it is appropriate. I certainly want to take this opportunity to repeat my thanks to those people who created any of the material which is not my own.

I particularly wish to single out Jerome and Thea Berryman whose labour of love over decades created the Godly Play method of storytelling which has been the inspiration for all of my work. At the core of Jerome and Thea's work is the wish to develop children's spirituality and religious language and whilst these stories do not try to proselytize, I do want to encourage everyone, adults and children, to utilise their participation in this method of storytelling to engage in awe and wonder deeply and make meaning for themselves.

I would like to thank those who offered to collaborate on parts of this book to help me navigate unknown aspects of some of the religious traditions I took stories from. Only by listening carefully to lived experience is it possible to truly deliver authentic material which respects each religious tradition.

Thanks, in particular, to: Molly Acharya, Katie Freeman, Katie Gooch and her work on Sidegate Multi-faith Reflective Story Project at Sidegate Primary School, Ipswich, Kathryn Lord, Juliet Lyal, Sukaina Manji, Naila Missous, Ed Pawson, Susie Peeler, Adam Robertson and Georgina Uttley.

Thanks to Ann Hobbs and the team at Forward Thinking Publishing who saw this book from rough draft through to publication and brought life to the idea I'd had in my head for about three years.

A huge debt of gratitude goes to all of the people who kindly donated to my GoFundMe campaign which financed the publication of this book. Every single one of you have made a difference. I can't describe in words what it means to have your support for this project.

Finally, my thanks go to my biggest fan; Mike, who is a constant source of encouragement and my solace when things get tricky. You always believe, always listen and always cheer me on.

About the Author

Katherine Taylor was born within the sound of Bow bells, East London. As a Cockney, and with Irish heritage, Katherine believes she is predisposed to be a great storyteller! Katherine is married to Mike and together they have three grown sons, an energetic bull lurcher called Fossey and a very lazy cat named Einstein.

Katherine lives in Somerset and, until very recently, worked in a village primary school delivering all of the R.E. there. She also delivers reflective storytelling in other primary and secondary settings, speaks at conferences, and delivers twilight training sessions at schools throughout Somerset, Dorset, Devon and Cornwall, and even further afield sometimes.

Katherine's passion is to see the Time to Wonder reflective storytelling method used with confidence by practitioners in school settings nationwide; to provide young people and their teachers with the time and space to be still and wonder deeply.

If you want to find out more about Katherine and her work, you'll find her on:

Twitter	@thetime2wonder
Instagram	thetime2wonder
Email	thetime2wonder@gmail.com
YouTube	thetime2wonder channel

Katherine's YouTube channel provides videos of every story in this book to help the reader get a better sense of material placement and pace.

Lightning Source UK Ltd.
Milton Keynes UK
UKHW052353070222
398314UK00016B/607